641.5

Simply steamed

Simply steamed

Isabel Brancq

Photographs by David Japy
Styling by Isabel Brancq

HACHETTE
Illustrated

Contrary to popular belief, steam cooking need not be bland. Steaming food is an easy, healthy but flavourful way of cooking which lends itself to any number of preparations, both traditional and innovative, and is often a very quick way of preparing food. For example, steaming peppers for marinating is much quicker than roasting them. Many ingredients, especially fish and vegetables, taste true and fresh when steamed – steamed spiced apples are a taste revelation, when compared to more conventional ways of cooking them.

In this book, you will find many inspiring recipes all prepared with a steamer. Most of them can also be made with a pressure cooker, and cooking times have been indicated at the bottom of the recipes (time to be counted from the point of boiling). To give your steamed foods even more flavour, try infusing the steaming water with herbs and spices, and keeping the seasonings light, opting for vinaigrettes and lemon juice in place of butter or cream.

The recipes can also be made in a double-bowl electric steamer. However, instead of infusing the steaming water with herbs and spices, put them into the steaming bowl below that contains the food to be flavoured. For casserole-type dishes, combine the ingredients in the 'rice' bowl (which comes as part of the electric steamer) and place that in a steaming bowl. Aluminium foil parcels, ramekins or moulds can be cooked in a steaming bowl.

Enjoy steaming and always remember to be creative with your cooking!

contents

Veal rolls with chicken and mustard

- Lay the veal escalopes flat on a work surface and pat dry with kitchen paper.
- Steam the chicken breasts for 10 minutes over water that has been flavoured with 2 sprigs of tarragon. Season to taste.
- Tear the bread into pieces and put in a food processor with the chicken and mustard. Process until blended.
- Spread some of the chicken mixture over each of the veal escalopes, roll up and secure with kitchen string. Arrange 8 sprigs of tarragon in the steamer basket and lay each veal roll on top of 2 sprigs.
- Steam for 15 minutes.

Serves 4
Preparation: 15 minutes
Cooking time: 25 minutes

4 veal escalopes
2 chicken breasts
1 bunch tarragon
3 slices bread
1 tablespoon Dijon mustard with tarragon
salt and pepper

Variations
Use different flavoured mustards, or add more ingredients to the stuffing, like chopped tomatoes or fresh coriander. You can also sprinkle some curry powder over the chicken breasts before steaming.

Tips
Serve with green vegetables, such as green beans or broccoli. If you are using frozen vegetables, do not cook for as long. Add tarragon to the vegetables, or other any other fresh herb you fancy.

Pressure cooker
Wrap each veal roll in aluminium foil and cook for 7 minutes.

Meatballs with coriander

Serves 4
Preparation: 20 minutes
Cooking time:
15 minutes

2 garlic cloves
2 shallots
600 g (1 lb 6 oz) minced beef
2 bunches of coriander, chopped
2 eggs, beaten
2 tablespoons tomato purée
5 tablespoons breadcrumbs
1 beef or chicken stock cube
salt and pepper

- Finely chop the garlic and shallots.
- In a bowl, break up the minced beef with a fork. Add the garlic, shallots, coriander, eggs, tomato purée and breadcrumbs, mixing well after each addition. Season with salt and pepper.
- With your hands, form the mixture into 16 balls, then steam for 15 minutes over boiling water that has been seasoned with a stock cube.

Variations

Combine the beef with other meats, such as chicken, spicy sausage or bacon. Replace the coriander with chervil or parsley and chopped prunes. You can also add 1 teaspoon capers, chopped anchovies or black olives. Try rolling the meatballs in cumin seeds, sesame seeds or crushed chilli before steaming. This dish also delicious cold, served with strips of pepper that have been steamed for 15 minutes, cooled and then drizzled with olive oil and sprinkled with thin slices of garlic and salt and pepper and been allowed to refrigerate for 1 hour.

Tips

Serve with potato or carrot purée.

Pressure cooker

Cook the meatballs in aluminium foil for 7 minutes.

Serves 4
Preparation: 10 minutes
Cooking time: 20 minutes

4 chicken thigh and drumstick joints
1 tablespoon curry powder
1 chicken stock cube
4 bananas, not too ripe

Quick curry-spiced chicken with banana

• Sprinkle the chicken with the curry powder. Bring the cooking water to the boil with the stock cube, then steam the chicken for 20 minutes.
• Cut the bananas into rounds and add to the chicken after 10 minutes.

Tips
Serve with basmati rice or steamed potatoes.

13

Chicken with curry mayonnaise

- Steam the chicken for 18 minutes. When cool, slice thinly.
- Split the almonds in half.
- Soak the sultanas in a bowl of warm water for 15 minutes, then drain.
- Peel the apples, then cut into small cubes.
- Rinse the coriander and strip the leaves.
- For the mayonnaise: whisk together the egg yolk, curry powder and mustard. Season with salt and pepper. Continue whisking vigorously, gradually pouring in the oil in a thin stream until the mixture thickens to the correct consistency. Taste for seasoning.
- Mix the chicken slices with the mayonnaise. Stir in the sultanas, apples, almonds and coriander.
- Serve with basmati rice or steamed potatoes.

Serves 4
Preparation: 10 minutes
Cooking time: 18 minutes

4 chicken breasts
50 g (2 oz) almonds
50 g (2 oz) sultanas
2 red apples
5 coriander sprigs

• For the mayonnaise:
1 egg yolk
pinch of curry powder
1 tablespoon mustard
150 ml (¼ pint) peanut or sunflower oil
salt and pepper

Variations

Sprinkle the chicken lightly with curry powder before steaming. Add some desiccated or fresh coconut shavings when combining the chicken with the mayonnaise, or try adding a slice of fresh root ginger to the water for steaming.

Chicken and broccoli salad

Serves 4
Preparation: 25 minutes
Cooking time: 30 minutes

500 g (1 lb) broccoli ● 4 chicken
or turkey breasts ● 1 chicken stock
cube ● 20 cherry tomatoes ● juice
of 1 lemon ● 2 tablespoons olive
oil ● 2 tablespoons chopped fresh
thyme ● 2 tablespoons olive oil
● salt and pepper

● Wash the broccoli, separate into florets and steam
for 20 minutes. Set aside to cool.

● Sprinkle the chicken or turkey with pepper. Bring the
cooking water to the boil with the stock cube, then
steam the chicken for 20 minutes. When
cool, cut into slices or small cubes.

● Wash the tomatoes and slice
into quarters.

● Whisk together the
lemon juice, olive
oil and thyme for
the dressing.

● Chop the
broccoli florets
if too large. In
a bowl, toss the
chicken with the
tomatoes, broccoli
and dressing. Season
with salt and pepper
and serve immediately.

Variations

Replace the broccoli with green beans or
shelled peas and add rice or pasta for a more
substantial salad. If you have a multi-tiered steamer,
cook the chicken and broccoli together, with the chicken
underneath the broccoli.

Chicken, rice and pineapple

● Sprinkle the chicken breasts with pepper. Bring the cooking water to the boil with the stock cube, then steam the chicken for 10 minutes. Allow to cool, then cut into slices or small cubes.

● Steam the rice for 15 minutes, stirring occasionally. Transfer to a bowl to cool.

● Peel the pineapple and cut into small cubes, then mix with the rice.

● Combine the yogurt and lime juice. Add the chicken, then the rice. Season with salt and pepper and serve.

Variations

Ready-made flavoured rice, such as coconut or saffron, can be used in place of ordinary rice, or use cooked pasta.

Serves 4
Preparation: 15 minutes
Cooking time: 35 minutes

4 chicken breasts
1 chicken stock cube
150 g (5 oz) long grain rice
1 small pineapple
2 tablespoons natural yogurt
juice of 1 lime
salt and pepper

Chicken parcels
with tarragon

Serves 4
Preparation: 15 minutes
Cooking time: 30 minutes

1 bunch large spring onions
5 tarragon sprigs
2 chicken thighs
2 chicken breasts
3 tablespoons olive oil
200 ml (7 fl oz) crème fraîche
1 chicken stock cube
salt and pepper

- Trim the onions and cut in half.
- Rinse the tarragon, then strip the leaves.
- Put the chicken pieces in a pan, along with the oil, tarragon and onions. Season with salt and pepper and cook until browned, about 3 minutes each side. Stir in the crème fraîche and remove from the heat.
- Prepare 4 sheets of aluminium foil. Put 1 chicken piece on each sheet, and divide the onion mixture equally between the 4 portions. Fold over and seal the foil parcels, then steam for 25 minutes over water that has been seasoned with the stock cube.
- Serve with green beans and fried potatoes.

21

Serves 4
Preparation: 15 minutes
Cooking time: 10 minutes

4 chicken breasts
100 g (3½ oz) mixed tender salad leaves
30 g (1 oz) rocket
5 sprigs each of flat leaf parsley,
chervil and chives
30 g (1 oz) sultanas
30 g (1 oz) hazelnuts

• **For the vinaigrette:**
3 tablespoons olive oil
1 tablespoon wine vinegar
salt and pepper

Chicken and herb salad

• Season the chicken with pepper, then steam for 10 minutes. When cool, cut into slices or cubes.
• Wash the salad leaves, rocket and the herbs and pat dry with a teatowel. Snip the herbs coarsely with scissors.
• In a large bowl, gently combine the chicken, salad leaves, rocket, herbs, sultanas and hazelnuts.
• For the vinaigrette: whisk together the oil and vinegar. Pour over the chicken salad, season with salt and pepper and toss well. Serve immediately.

Variations

For more flavour and colour, add a few nasturtium flowers, which are available from specialist green-grocers. Croûtons also make a pleasant addition.

23

Chicory with ham

- Trim the chicory and rinse. Halve lengthways and core, leaving 8 sets of large outer leaves.
- Cut the ham into small pieces.
- For the white sauce: melt the butter in a small pan. Stir in the flour, mix well, then gradually pour in the milk, stirring constantly, until thick. Season with salt, pepper and nutmeg.
- Stir the ham pieces into the white sauce. Divide the mixture into 4 halves of the chicory leaves and sprinkle with some grated cheese. Season and close up with the remaining leaves. Secure with cocktail sticks or kitchen string.
- Steam the stuffed chicory leaves for 15 minutes, then remove the cocktail sticks or string. Serve immediately.

Variations

Use Parmesan in place of the Gruyère. You can also stir some cumin seeds into the white sauce, or replace the ham with slices of smoked duck breast.

Tip

Use the leftover chicory hearts in a salad.

Serves 4
Preparation: 15 minutes
Cooking time: 15 minutes

4 chicory
4 ham slices
55 g (2 oz) Gruyère cheese, grated

- **For the white sauce:**
50 g (2 oz) unsalted butter
50 g (2 oz) flour
250 ml (8 fl oz) milk
pinch of grated nutmeg
salt and pepper

Serves 4
Preparation: 10 minutes
Cooking time: 8 minutes

2 leeks, white part only
3 shallots, finely chopped
8 scallops
pinch of ground turmeric
salt and pepper

Scallops with leeks

• Wash the leeks and cut into thin slices. Mix the shallots with the leeks.
• Steam the vegetables for 5 minutes, then season.
• Place the scallops on top of the vegetables, sprinkle with turmeric and continue steaming for 3 more minutes. Serve immediately.

Variations
Drizzle the scallops with melted butter, enclose in aluminium foil parcels and steam.

Tips
These quantities are for a starter. If you prefer to serve this dish as a main course, allow 3 scallops per person and serve with rice.

Cod with tomatoes and garlic

- Place each cod fillet on a sheet of aluminium foil.
- Peel the garlic and slice thinly.
- Wash the cherry tomatoes and cut in half.
- Arrange 4 tomato halves on each of the cod fillets and top the tomatoes with a slice of garlic. Drizzle over some olive oil and season with salt and pepper. Fold over the aluminium foil and seal the parcel tightly.
- Steam for 15 minutes.
- Serve in the parcel with pasta or ratatouille.

Serves 4
Preparation: 10 minutes
Cooking time: 15 minutes

4 cod fillets
1 garlic clove
8 cherry tomatoes
olive oil
salt and pepper

Cod rolls
with cheese

- Place the cod fillets on a flat plate or board. Season with salt and pepper.
- Cut the cheese into small cubes.
- Put a few cubes of cheese on top of each fillet, then roll up the fillet (starting at the thin end) to enclose the cheese. Secure firmly with cocktail sticks or kitchen string.
- Scrub the orange. Remove 4 strips of rind with a vegetable peeler and put in the cooking water. Squeeze the juice from the orange and set aside.
- Arrange the cod rolls in the steamer basket and pour over the orange juice.
- Steam for 15 minutes, sprinkle with sesame seeds and serve immediately.

Variation
Use a mild Cheddar in place of the Gruyère cheese.

Tips
Serve with an chicory and orange salad and steamed new potatoes.

Serves 4
Preparation: 15 minutes
Cooking time: 15 minutes

4 cod fillets
120 g (4 oz) Gruyère cheese
1 orange
1 teaspoon sesame seeds
salt and pepper

Cod in ramekins with yogurt sauce

- Season the cod with salt and pepper, then steam for 10 minutes. Flake.
- Meanwhile, put the milk in a saucepan with the fennel seeds and warm gently. Strain the milk to remove the fennel seeds and pour over the bread. Allow to stand for 15 minutes. Squeeze the milk out of the bread.
- In a bowl, gradually combine the flaked fish fillets, bread and eggs. Season with salt and pepper. Pour into 4 buttered ramekin moulds and cover with aluminium foil.
- Steam for 20 minutes. Let cool, then unmould.
- Wash the chives, snip with scissors and stir into the yogurt.
- Serve the fish warm, accompanied by the yogurt sauce.

Tips
Serve with rice or toast.

Serves 4
Preparation: 20 minutes
Cooking time: 30 minutes

400 g (13 oz) cod or haddock fillets
100 ml (3½ fl oz) milk
1 teaspoon fennel seeds
150 g (5 oz) sliced bread, crusts trimmed
2 eggs
40 g (1½ oz) unsalted butter
5 chives
1 small pot natural yogurt
salt and pepper

Hake stuffed with crab and prawns

Serves 4
Preparation: 10 minutes
Cooking time: 10 minutes

8 thin hake fillets
2 limes
1 small can crab meat
1 small can prawns
salt and pepper

- Place the hake fillets on a large plate or board and season with salt and pepper.
- Wash 1 of the limes and peel 4 strips of rind with a vegetable peeler. Put the strips of lime rind in the water for steaming.
- Divide the crab meat and prawns between the hake fillets. Squeeze a little lime juice over each, season, then roll up (starting from the thin end) to enclose the crab and prawns. Secure with cocktail sticks or kitchen string.
- Steam for 10 minutes, then remove the cocktail sticks or string.
- Serve with basmati rice or fresh pasta.

Variations

Use smoked salmon in place of the crab, or mix finely chopped sun-dried tomatoes with the crab meat. You can adapt this recipe to suit the season, or your fancy.

Tips

This dish is also delicious served cold, with a dollop of mayonnaise. Use any leftover crab and prawns to make a seafood salad with some grapefruit and orange slices.

Salmon and leek en papillote

- Wash the salmon and pat dry.
- Wash the leeks and cut into rounds or thin strips.
- Peel the carrots and cut into thin rounds.
- Steam all the vegetables together for 5 minutes.
- Butter 4 pieces of aluminium foil and put 1 piece of salmon in the middle of each sheet. Season with salt and pepper. Divide the vegetable mixture between the 4 salmon steaks and top each with a slice of lemon. Fold over the aluminium foil to enclose the salmon and seal well.
- Steam for 20 minutes.
- To make the sauce: combine the butter and shallots in a pan and cook until soft, about 5 minutes. Stir in the wine and cream, then simmer gently for around 15 minutes. Season with salt and pepper.
- To serve, open the salmon parcels and pour some sauce over each. Serve immediately.

Pressure cooker
Cook the parcels for 7 minutes.

Serves 4
Preparation: 15 minutes
Cooking time: 25 minutes

4 salmon steaks
2 leeks, white part only
2 carrots
50 g (2 oz) unsalted butter
4 lemon slices
salt and pepper

- **For the sauce:**
30 g (1 oz) unsalted butter
2 shallots, chopped
250 ml (8 fl oz) dry white wine
200 ml (7 fl oz) double cream

Salmon with dill
and potatoes

- Wash the salmon fillets and pat dry.
- Wash the dill and chop all but 1 sprig finely.
- Peel the potatoes, then cut into thin slices. Combine the potato slices, half the dill and some salt and pepper.
- Bring the wine and some water to the boil with the remaining sprig of dill. Arrange the seasoned potato slices in the steamer basket and place the salmon on top. Steam for 20 minutes. Serve immediately.

Tip
Pour in the wine before adding the water so you can adjust the level to suit your steamer.

Pressure cooker
Wrap in nonstick baking parchment and cook in a pressure cooker for 10 minutes.

Serves 4
Preparation: 15 minutes
Cooking time: 20 minutes

4 salmon fillets
1 bunch of dill
700 g (1½ lb) new potatoes
350 ml (12 fl oz) dry white wine
salt and pepper

Tuna steaks
with peppers

- Cut each pepper in half, lengthwise. Remove the core and seeds, then slice. Steam for 20 minutes. Arrange the red pepper slices on a large, flat plate. When cool, drizzle with olive oil and slices of garlic. Season with salt and pepper and refrigerate for 1 hour.
- Steam the tuna steaks until cooked, about 10-15 minutes.
- Serve the tuna hot or cold, with the marinated peppers.

Variation

Combine 1 teaspoon finely chopped capers with 100 g (3½ oz) softened unsalted butter and serve with the tuna.

Tip

Tuna can be served slightly rare, so adjust the cooking time to suit your taste.

Serves 4
Preparation: 15 minutes
Cooking time:
30-35 minutes
Chilling time: 1 hour

2 red peppers
olive oil
1 garlic clove, peeled and sliced
4 tuna steaks
(about 200 g/7 oz each)
salt and pepper

Salmon and cucumber salad

- Rinse the salmon fillets and pat dry. Steam for 15 minutes, then allow to cool.
- Wash and peel the cucumber. Cut in half lengthways, deseed, then dice. Steam for 10 minutes, drain, then leave to cool in a shallow bowl.
- In a large bowl, combine the yogurt, vinegar, dill and pepper. Drain the cucumber cubes, then add to the yogurt dressing and mix well.
- Slice the salmon fillets and stir into the cucumber mixture. Cover and refrigerate for at least 2 hours before serving.

Variations
You can add croutons to the salad, or try serving it with pasta.

Pressure cooker
Make 4 nonstick baking parchment parcels with the salmon and cucumber combined and cook for 7 minutes. Allow to cool, then drizzle with the yogurt dressing.

Serves 4
Preparation: 15 minutes
Cooking time: 25 minutes
Chilling time: 2 hours

4 small salmon fillets
1 cucumber
2 small pots of natural yogurt
1 tablespoon wine vinegar
1 teaspoon finely chopped dill
1 teaspoon pepper

Skate, grapefruit and rice salad

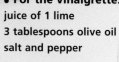

Serves 4
Preparation: 15 minutes
Cooking time: 20 minutes

200 g (7 oz) long grain rice
2 small skate wings
3 pink grapefruit

● For the vinaigrette:
juice of 1 lime
3 tablespoons olive oil
salt and pepper

- Rinse the rice, then steam for 20 minutes.
- Wash the skate wings and add them to the steamer basket above the rice. Cook together for 15 minutes.
- Place the skate on a plate and allow to cool.
- Rinse the rice under cold, running water, drain well, then put in a large bowl.
- Using a small knife, slice the top and bottom from each grapefruit, then cut away the peel with all the pith to expose the flesh. Use the knife to ease the segments out from each membrane.
- Combine the rice with the grapefruit segments and mix gently. Remove the bones from the skate then add the fish to the rice mixture.
- For the vinaigrette: whisk together the lime juice and oil and season well. Pour over the salad, mix well and serve.

Variations

Use other citrus fruits in place of the grapefruit. Use flavoured rice or mix several different types of rice together.

44

Salad Niçoise
with fresh tuna

● Rinse the rice, then steam for 20 minutes, stirring occasionally. Allow to cool.

● While steaming the rice, place the green beans in another level of the steamer and cook for 12 minutes. Allow to cool, then halve the beans.

● Steam the tuna for 10-15 minutes, then cut into large cubes.

● Boil the eggs for 10 minutes, peel and quarter.

● Wash and quarter the tomatoes.

● In a large bowl, combine the rice, green beans, tuna, hard-boiled eggs, tomatoes and black olives. Season with salt and pepper.

● To make the vinaigrette: whisk together the vinegar and oil, pour over the salad and toss well. Serve immediately.

Tip

Tuna can be served slightly rare, so adjust the cooking time to suit your taste.

Serves 4
Preparation:
25 minutes
Cooking time:
40-45 minutes

200 g (7 oz) long grain rice
200 g (7 oz) green beans
250 g (9 oz) fresh tuna
3 eggs
4 tomatoes
150 g (5 oz) pitted black olives
salt and pepper

● **For the vinaigrette:**
3 tablespoons wine vinegar
6 tablespoons olive oil

48

Sauerkraut with fish

• Put the sauerkraut in a colander and rinse under cold running water, tossing with your hands. Press down with your hands to extract all the water.

• Put the sauerkraut and juniper berries in a steamer basket and steam for 45 minutes. Pour over half of the wine, pouring slowly at first so that the steaming water does not overflow.

• Meanwhile, peel the potatoes and halve if they are large.

• Cut the monkfish into pieces.

• For the sauce: cut the butter into small pieces. Peel the shallots and chop finely. Cook them in the remaining wine, until the liquid is reduced by half. Remove from the heat and stir in the butter, whisking well. Season with salt and pepper and add the lemon juice.

• Add the potatoes to the sauerkraut and cook for a further 30 minutes. Add the monkfish, haddock and mackerel and cook for another 15 minutes. Add the eel and cook for 5 minutes more.

• Arrange the sauerkraut, potatoes and fish on a serving platter. Place the sauce in a serving dish and serve.

Tip
Ready-made sauerkraut can be used in place of fresh, in which case it should be added when cooking the fish, just to warm it through. Adjust the quantity to suit.

Serves 4
Preparation: 30 minutes
Cooking time: 1 hour 35 minutes

1.5 kg (3½ lb) raw sauerkraut • 10 juniper berries • 1 bottle Alsatian Riesling • 6 potatoes • 400 g (14 oz) monkfish • 1 smoked haddock fillet • 1 smoked mackerel • 4 smoked eel slices • **For the sauce:** 200 g (7 oz) unsalted butter • 2 shallots • 2 tablespoons lemon juice • salt and pepper

Serves 4
Preparation: 15 minutes
Cooking time: 30 minutes

1 large fennel bulb
4 small sea bream fillets
(about 200 g/7 oz each)
2 onions
2 garlic cloves
1 tablespoon olive oil
1 celery stick
3 thyme sprigs
2 bay leaves
salt and pepper

Sea bream with fennel

- Wash the fennel and slice.
- Rinse the fish fillets.
- Arrange the fennel slices in a steamer basket, lay the fish on top and steam until cooked.
- Meanwhile, slice the onions and crush the garlic. Heat the oil in a pan, add the onions and garlic and cook until soft.
- Wash the celery and chop. Add to the onion mixture, along with the thyme and bay leaves. Stir well and continue cooking for another 10 minutes.
- When the fish is cooked arrange the fillets on 4 plates. Top with the fennel mixture, season with salt and pepper and serve immediately.

Tip
Serve with steamed potatoes and chicory and celery salad.

Serves 4
Preparation: 15 minutes
Cooking time: 15 minutes

**4 large red mullets, cleaned
and scaled (or 8 fillets)**
1 lime
1 cucumber
1 garlic clove
1 small pot of natural yogurt
salt and pepper

Red mullet with yogurt
and cucumber sauce

- Wash the red mullets.
- Scrub the lime. With a vegetable peeler, remove 2 long strips of rind from the lime and add these to the water used for steaming.
- Cut 4 lime slices and stuff 1 inside each red mullet.
- Steam the fish for 15 minutes.
- Meanwhile, wash and peel the cucumber. Slice lengthwise into 4 long strips, deseed, then cut into small cubes.
- Peel the garlic and slice thinly.
- In a small bowl, stir together the garlic, yogurt and cucumber. Season to taste with salt and pepper. Refrigerate until needed.
- When the red mullet are cooked, serve with the cucumber salad and toast.

Skate with capers

- Rinse the skate wings, then steam for 15 minutes.
- Meanwhile, melt the butter in a pan over low heat. Stir in the capers.
- Arrange the skate wings on 4 plates, pour over the warm caper sauce and serve immediately.

Variations

If you want to omit the butter, simply steam the skate with the capers on top and serve. Tapenade (black olive paste) can be used in place of the capers. Basil butter can be made by replacing the capers with a handful of snipped fresh basil leaves.

Tips

Skate goes off very quickly so be sure it is fresh when purchased and cook it on the same day. Skate can also be eaten cold in salad.

Serves 4
Preparation: 5 minutes
Cooking time: 15 minutes

2 small skate wings
50 g (2 oz) unsalted butter
50 g (2 oz) capers

Serves 4
Preparation: 15 minutes
Cooking time: 30 minutes

200 g (7 oz) fresh, or frozen, peas • **5 carrots** • **16 large cooked prawns**
For the vinaigrette: juice of 1 lime • 3 tablespoons olive oil • salt and pepper

Pea, carrot and prawn salad

• Shell the peas. Wash the carrots, peel and cut into thin rounds.

• Put the carrots in a steamer basket and steam for 20 minutes. Put the peas in another basket and steam for 12 minutes (reduce time if using frozen peas). Allow to cool, then toss the vegetables together and season with salt and pepper.

• Remove the prawn heads, then add the prawns to the vegetables and mix well.

• For the vinaigrette: whisk together the lime juice, oil and salt and pepper to taste. Pour over the salad, toss well and serve.

Tip
This is also delicious served warm with grilled or steamed prawn kebabs.

Pressure cooker
To cook the vegetables in a pressure cooker, allow 5 minutes for fresh peas and 7 minutes for the carrots.

Fish mousse
with broccoli

- Wash the broccoli, separate into florets and steam for 10 minutes. Rinse under cold water, drain and set aside.
- In a food processor, combine the fish, eggs, potato flour, crème fraîche and onion. Season with salt and pepper. Mix well, cover and refrigerate for 30 minutes.
- Put the broccoli in the food processor and purée. Stir into the cold fish mixture.
- Butter 4 ramekins and fill with the fish mixture. Cover with aluminium foil and steam for 30 minutes. Let cool, then refrigerate for 6 hours.
- For the sauce: cook the onion in the oil until soft. Cut the tomatoes into eighths and add to the onion, along with the thyme and basil leaves. Stir well. Add the sugar and season with salt and pepper to taste. Mix well, then simmer gently for 15 minutes. Put in a food processor and purée. Refrigerate until needed.
- To serve, pour some sauce over each ramekin and accompany with toast.

Variations
Use peppers, green beans or peas in place of the broccoli, or alternate layers of different vegetables (cabbage, carrots, etc) for a more colourful presentation.

Serves 4
Preparation: 20 minutes
Cooking time: 40 minutes
Chilling time: 6 hours

150 g (5 oz) broccoli
250 g (8 oz) fish fillets, such as haddock
2 eggs
1 tablespoon potato flour
2 tablespoons crème fraîche
1 tablespoon finely chopped onion

- **For the sauce:**
1 onion, finely chopped
1 tablespoon olive oil
200 g (7 oz) tomatoes
leaves from 3 fresh thyme sprigs
10 fresh basil leaves
1 teaspoon sugar
salt and pepper

Rice salad with green beans and peppers

- Wash the peppers. Deseed, core and cut into small cubes.
- Rinse the rice, then steam for 20 minutes, stirring occasionally.
- Trim the green beans and steam in a basket set above the rice for 12 minutes. When the rice and green beans have cooled, put them in a bowl with the peppers.
- For the vinaigrette: whisk together all the ingredients, and season well with salt and pepper.
- Pour the vinaigrette over the salad, toss well and refrigerate for 1 hour before serving.

Variation
The peppers can also be steamed as an alternative to using them raw.

Tips
To save time, use canned green beans. If using frozen green beans, steam for 5 minutes.

Pressure cooker
Cook the green beans for 6 minutes.

Serves 4
Preparation: 10 minutes
Cooking time: 30 minutes
Chilling time: 1 hour

3 red or yellow peppers
150 g (5 oz) long grain rice
200g (7 oz) green beans

- **For the vinaigrette:**
1 teaspoon Dijon mustard with tarragon
2 tablespoons wine vinegar
4 tablespoons olive oil
salt and pepper

Steamed potatoes
with chive cream

- Peel the potatoes, cut into quarters lengthways and season to taste with salt and pepper. Steam for 20 minutes.
- Rinse and drain the chives.
- Put the crème fraîche into a bowl and, with scissors, snip the chives into the bowl. Stir well together and season to taste. Cover and refrigerate.
- Serve the steamed potatoes with the chive cream.

Variations

Use parsley in place of the chives. Butter flavoured with walnuts, almonds, fresh thyme or tarragon can be used in place of the chive cream. Simply combine 100 g (3½ oz) softened unsalted butter with the ingredient of your choice, finely ground or chopped.

Pressure cooker

Steam the potatoes for 12 minutes.

Serves 4
Preparation: 15 minutes
Cooking time: 20 minutes

1 kg (2 lb) boiling potatoes
1 bunch of chives
250 ml (8 fl oz) crème fraîche
salt and white pepper

63

Serves 4
Preparation: 10 minutes
Cooking time: 10 minutes

1 kg (2 lb) carrots
1 bunch of coriander
salt and pepper

Carrots with coriander

- Peel the carrots and slice into thin rounds.
- Rinse and chop the coriander, mix with the carrots, season with salt and pepper and steam for 10 minutes.

Variations
The steamed carrots may be puréed, or used as a base for carrot and coriander soup. 1 teaspoon of ground coriander can be used in place of fresh coriander.

Pressure cooker
Steam for 5 minutes.

Steamed peas
with bacon

- Rinse the herbs.
- Shell the peas and put in a steamer basket with the bacon and herbs. Steam for 12 minutes.

Tips

If using frozen peas, reduce the cooking time of the peas only to 5 minutes. This makes an ideal accompaniment for roast pork or an omelette.

Pressure cooker

Steam for 5 minutes.

Serves 4
Preparation: 15 minutes
Cooking time: 12 minutes

3 tarragon sprigs
3 chervil sprigs
500 g (1 lb) fresh peas
150 g (5 oz) bacon, cut into strips

Serves 4
Preparation: 15 minutes
Cooking time: 20 minutes

4 red and yellow peppers
1 small fresh goat's cheese
1 tablespoon olive oil
5 chives, snipped
salt and pepper

Pepper rolls with goat's cheese

- Wash the peppers and cut each in half. Remove the core and seeds and cut into wide strips. Steam for 20 minutes.
- In a bowl, mix the cheese, oil and snipped chives. Season with salt and pepper to taste.
- When the peppers have cooled, top each slice with some of the cheese mixture and roll up to enclose (the peppers skins can be removed first if you prefer). Secure the rolls with cocktail sticks. Arrange on a plate and serve.

Variations
A variety of different coloured peppers is more appealing. The steamed strips can be filled with any number of mixtures. Ready-made tapenade (black olive paste) is an easy alternative. Crab mixed with mayonnaise is also tasty.

Couscous salad with green beans and chickpeas

- Rinse the couscous and then steam for 10 minutes.
- Trim the green beans, place in another steamer basket and steam over the couscous for 12 minutes. Allow the couscous and green beans to cool, put in a bowl, add the chickpeas and mix well.
- Rinse and dry the parsley. Snip with scissors into the couscous mixture.
- For the dressing: whisk together the oil and lemon juice, adjusting the lemon juice to taste. Season with salt and pepper. Add to the salad, toss well and refrigerate for at least 1 hour.

Variations
Add chopped yellow and orange peppers, fresh or sun-dried tomatoes, chopped fresh figs, diced cooked chicken or turkey, or melon balls.

Tip
Frozen green beans can be used in place of fresh, in which case reduce steaming time of the beans to 5 minutes.

Pressure cooker
Steam fresh green beans for 6 minutes.

Serves 4
Preparation: 25 minutes
Cooking time: 20 minutes
Chilling time: 1 hour

150 g (5 oz) couscous ● 300 g (10 oz) green beans ● 1 small can chickpeas, rinsed and drained ● 1 bunch of flat leaf parsley ● **For the dressing:** juice of 2 lemons ● 3 tablespoons olive oil ● salt and pepper

Artichokes with tomato basil sauce

- Wash the artichokes and trim the stems. Steam for 35 minutes.
- Meanwhile, prepare the tomato sauce. Peel the onion and slice. Heat the oil in a pan, add the sliced onion and cook until soft.
- Wash the tomatoes and cut each one in half. Remove the seeds, then cut into small cubes. Add to the onions and simmer gently for 15 minutes. Season with salt and pepper to taste.
- Wash the basil, chop and add to the tomato mixture.
- When the artichokes are cooked, remove the leaves and fuzzy choke. Slice the hearts into pieces and stir in to the tomato sauce.
- Serve with toast.

Tips

The leaves can be eaten separately, dipped into olive oil or vinaigrette.

Pressure cooker

Cook the artichokes for 18 minutes.

Serves 4
Preparation: 15 minutes
Cooking time: 50 minutes

4 globe artichokes
- **For the sauce: 1 onion** - 1 tablespoon olive oil - 4 large tomatoes - 6 large basil leaves - salt and pepper

Mixed vegetables with herb butter

- Peel the potatoes and slice into thin rounds.
- Wash and trim the beans.
- Peel the onions and slice into rounds.
- Wash the tomatoes and slice into rounds.
- Rinse the herbs and pat dry. Reserve 1 sprig of each, then chop the rest finely.
- Put the whole herb sprigs into the water for steaming. Steam all the vegetables: 12 minutes for the beans, 20 minutes for the potatoes, 10 minutes for the onions and tomatoes. Season with salt and pepper to taste.
- Stir the chopped herbs into the butter.
- Serve the vegetables with the herb butter.

Variation

Add some Gorgonzola or blue cheese to the herb butter.

Pressure cooker

Put the potatoes in first, then the beans, onions and lastly the tomatoes, sprinkling some herbs between each layer. Cook for 15 minutes.

Serves 6
Preparation: 25 minutes
Cooking time: 40 minutes

500 g (1 lb) potatoes
500 g (1 lb) yellow or green beans
2 onions
500 g (1 lb) tomatoes
1 bunch of tarragon
1 bunch of coriander
**100 g (3½ oz) unsalted butter,
softened**
salt and pepper

Artichoke hearts with mushrooms

Serves 4
Preparation: 20 minutes
Cooking time: 1 hour

4 globe artichokes
1 tablespoon olive oil
100 g (3½ oz) smoked bacon, chopped
2 onions, chopped
3 tomatoes
200 g (7 oz) mushrooms
juice of 1 lemon
6 tablespoons dry white wine
salt and pepper

- Wash the artichokes and trim the stems. Steam for 35 minutes.
- Meanwhile, heat the oil in a pan. Add the bacon and onions and cook until golden.
- Wipe the mushrooms and cut into halves. Wash the tomatoes, deseed and cut into cubes.
- Toss the mushrooms with lemon juice, then add to the bacon mixture. Cook over low heat for 5 minutes. Add the tomatoes and wine. Season to taste with salt and pepper and simmer gently for 20 minutes.
- Remove the outer leaves of the artichokes and the fuzzy chokes. Pour the tomato sauce over the artichoke hearts.
- Serve with toast.

Tips
The leaves can be eaten separately, dipped into olive oil or vinaigrette.

Pressure cooker
Cook the artichokes for 18 minutes.

Broccoli with green sauce

Serves 4
Preparation: 20 minutes
Cooking time: 15 minutes

800 g (1³/₄ lb) broccoli

● **For the sauce:**
1 egg yolk
1 tablespoon Dijon mustard
300 ml (½ pint) peanut oil
1 tablespoon chopped chives
1 tablespoon chopped tarragon
1 tablespoon chopped chervil
1 tablespoon chopped capers

● Wash the broccoli and separate into florets. Steam for 15 minutes then drain well.

● Meanwhile prepare the sauce: put the egg yolk and mustard in a bowl and whisk. Gradually add the oil in a thin stream, whisking constantly until thick. Stir in the chopped herbs and capers.

● Serve the broccoli warm, accompanied by the herb sauce.

Variations

This sauce is also delicious with cold poultry or fish. Other vegetables may be used alongside the broccoli, such as carrot sticks or cauliflower.

Pressure cooker

Steam the broccoli for 5 minutes.

Asparagus with orange sauce

- Wash the asparagus and trim the ends. Steam for 15 minutes.
- To prepare the sauce: scrub the orange, peel strips of the rind with a vegetable peeler and then squeeze, retaining the juice.
- In a pan, combine the vinegar, 1 pinch of salt and pepper. Cook over a medium heat until reduced by half. Remove from the heat, and add 1 tablespoon water, the remaining pinch of salt and the egg yolks. Whisk well, then return to a low heat, whisking constantly.
- When the mixture begins to thicken, gradually add the butter pieces, the orange juice and the rinds. Stir and mix thoroughly before straining through a fine sieve.
- Serve the asparagus accompanied by the warm sauce.

Variation
Replace the orange juice with the juice of ½ pink grapefruit.

Pressure cooker
Cook the asparagus for 5 minutes.

Serves 4
Preparation: 20 minutes
Cooking time: 15 minutes

**20 white asparagus spears
(or enough for 4)**

- **For the sauce:**
**1 blood orange
2 tablespoons wine vinegar
4 egg yolks
200 g (7 oz) unsalted butter,
cut in small pieces
2 pinches salt
1 pinch ground white pepper**

Apples stuffed with dried fruit

Serves 4
Preparation: 20 minutes
Cooking time: 20 minutes

4 Golden Delicious apples
100 g (3½ oz) pitted dates
50 g (2 oz) chopped hazelnuts
3 tablespoons orange juice
1 tablespoon orange marmalade
6 tablespoons crème fraîche or whipping cream
1 tablespoon icing sugar

- Wash the apples and core. Make a criss-cross cut in the base.
- Chop the dates and mix with the hazelnuts, orange juice and marmalade. Fill the centre of each apple with the date mixture and steam for 20 minutes.
- Meanwhile, stir together the cream and sugar, then beat until frothy.
- Arrange the apples on plates, pour over the cream and serve.

Variations
Add 1 teaspoon cinnamon or vanilla sugar to the cream sauce.

Tip
If you season the apples with salt before steaming, they can be served as a savoury accompaniment for chicken or duck.

Pressure cooker
Wrap each apple in aluminium foil and cook for 10 minutes.

Steamed apples with raspberry mousse

- Wash the apples and core. Make a criss-cross cut in the base. Place each apple on a sheet of aluminium foil.
- Mix 1 tablespoon of the sugar with the ground almonds and sprinkle into the centre of each apple. Enclose the apples in the aluminium foil and seal well. Steam for 30 minutes.
- In a pan, combine the raspberries and the remaining sugar over low heat and cook for 10 minutes, squashing the raspberries with a fork.
- Whisk the egg white until firm, then fold carefully into the raspberries.
- Toast the brioche slices.
- Serve the apples warm, with a slice of toasted brioche and some raspberry mousse.

Variations
Replace the raspberries with redcurrants or blackberries. Butter the brioche slices before serving.

Tips
Keep a few whole raspberries for decoration. A good-quality raspberry jam can be used in place of the fresh raspberries.

Pressure cooker
Cook the apples for 10 minutes.

Serves 4
Preparation: 15 minutes
Cooking time: 40 minutes

4 apples, such as Gala or Golden Delicious
115 g (4 oz) sugar
50 g (2 oz) ground almonds
100 g (3½ oz) raspberries
1 egg white
4 brioche slices

Melting apples
with cinnamon

- Soak the raisins in warm water for 15 minutes, then drain.
- Peel the apples and cut into largish pieces.
- Sprinkle the apple pieces with cinnamon and sugar. Add the raisins and mix well.
- Put the cinnamon stick in the cooking water and steam the apple mixture for 15 minutes. Serve warm.

Variations

Pears and plums can also be added, as well as hazelnuts or almonds.

You can also use the fruit mixture as the filling for a large turnover: roll out a sheet of ready-made puff pastry and place on a baking tray. Spread the mixture down the middle and fold the dough over to enclose. Seal the edges of the dough, brush the top with beaten egg yolk and bake at 180°C (350°F), gas mark 4 for 15 minutes. Serve warm, with whipped cream.

Pressure cooker

Cook the apples in aluminium foil parcels for 6 minutes.

Serves 4
Preparation: 15 minutes
Cooking time: 15 minutes

100 g (3½ oz) raisins
1 kg (2 lb) apples, such as Gala or Golden Delicious
2 teaspoons ground cinnamon
1 tablespoon muscovado sugar
1 cinnamon stick

Banana parcels

- Peel the bananas and cut into rounds.
- In a bowl, combine the jam, coconut and lime juice. Mix well.
- Divide the bananas between 4 sheets of aluminium foil and spread the jam mixture on top. Close up the parcels and seal tightly. Steam for 10 minutes.
- Allow to cool completely before serving.

Variations
Serve with French toast. Use apricot jam in place of the redcurrant.

Pressure cooker
Cook the parcels for 4 minutes.

Serves 4
Preparation: 5 minutes
Cooking time: 10 minutes

4 bananas
3 tablespoons redcurrant jam
3 tablespoons desiccated coconut
juice of 2 limes

Serves 4
Preparation: 20 minutes
Cooking time: 20 minutes
Resting time: 1 hour

1 pineapple
4 bananas
1 ripe mango
2 pink grapefruit
10 fresh mint leaves, snipped with scissors
4 lime slices

Tropical fruit compote

- Peel the pineapple, bananas and mango. Cut the flesh into pieces. Steam together for 20 minutes. Allow to cool.
- Squeeze the grapefruit, then stir the mint into the juice. Pour over the fruit and mix well. Top with the lime slices and refrigerate for 1 hour before serving.

Variations

You can try adding some raisins, coconut slices and 1 tablespoon of dark rum, or slice a starfruit and add it to the fruit.

Pressure cooker

Cook the fruit in aluminium foil parcels for 10 minutes.

Index of recipes

Index of ingredients

Acknowledgements

- Many thanks to Carine for reading the recipes with her usual meticulous care, and for all her comments.
- Many thanks to Jacquard Français for the household linen, to Maison Staub for the pans, and to Compagnie Française de l'Orient et de la Chine for the plates and dishes.

Editorial director: Brigitte Éveno

Editorial assistant: Anne la Fay

Graphic design: Nicole Dassonville

Layout: Marie Vendittelli & Philippe Latombe

Photography: David Japy

Stylist: Isabel Brancq

Production: Claire Leleu

Translation: JMS Books LLP

© 2003 Hachette Livre (Hachette Pratique)
This edition © 2004 Hachette Illustrated UK, Octopus Publishing Group Ltd.,
2–4 Heron Quays, London E14 4JP

English translation by JMS Books LLP (email: moseleystrachan@blueyonder.co.uk)
Translation © Octopus Publishing Group

A CIP catalogue for this book is available from the British Library

ISBN: 1 84430 057 9

Printed in Singapore by Tien Wah Press